DANIEL the Dragon Saves the Day

RANDY PAGEL

PAGE PUBLISHING
Conneaut Lake, PA

First originally published by Page Publishing 2023

Original Art and Transcript by Randy Pagel

ISBN 978-1-6624-8679-1 (pbk)
ISBN 978-1-6624-8698-2 (digital)

Printed in the United States of America

Learn the letters of the alphabet
with Daniel the Dragon as we
follow his adventures with his
new family: the Andersons.

There is Daddy—Alex
and Mommy—Alexandra.

Their names start with the letter

A A a

And they have two children—their daughter *Briana* and their son *Brandon*.

Their names start with the letter

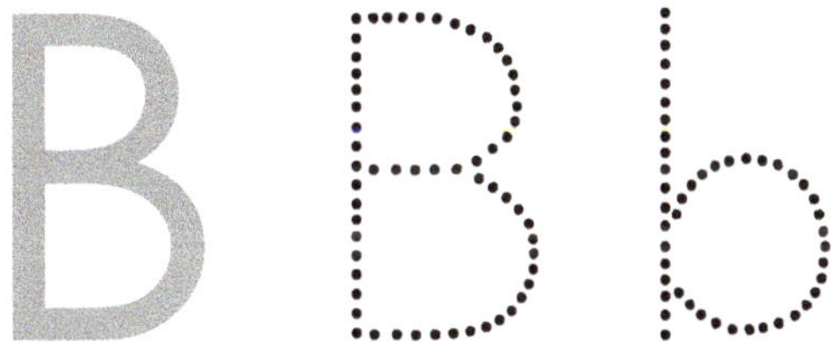

They are all one happy family.

So one day, they decided to build a pool in the backyard. The tractor man came, and as he was digging, he noticed a large egg in his shovel.

The man called the Andersons and
told them what he found. At first, they
all thought it was a Chicken egg. So
they asked if they could keep it.

"As long as you take Care of it," they said.

They kept it under lights to keep
it warm and help it grow.

The words *Chicken* and *Care*
start with the letter

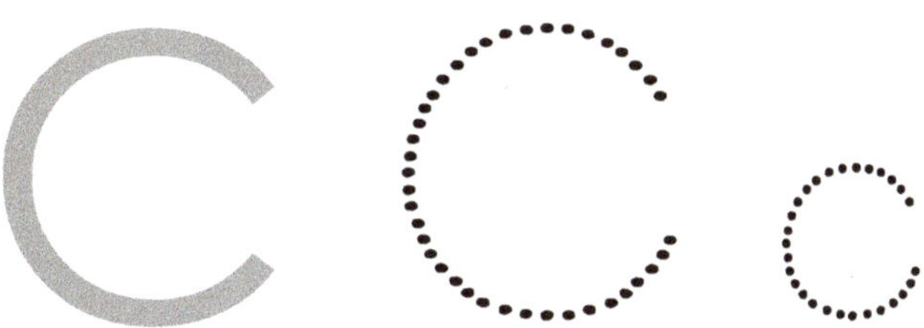

12

The egg grew and grew, and one day, the eggs started to break open. To their surprise…it was a baby dragon!

He grew into a big dragon very quickly.

YUM.

Daniel was very helpful with the chores.
He helped Mommy bake some Cookies.

And he helped daddy wash his Car.

What other words start with a

Daniel played *Dodgeball* with Brandon.

And he played teeter-totter with Brianna.

The words *Dodgeball* and
Daniel start with the letter

I HAVE AN IDEA.

One day, Daniel asked if we could go camping and *Enjoy* the outdoors.

So they packed up the car with good things to *Eat*.

The words *Enjoy* and *Eat* start with the letter

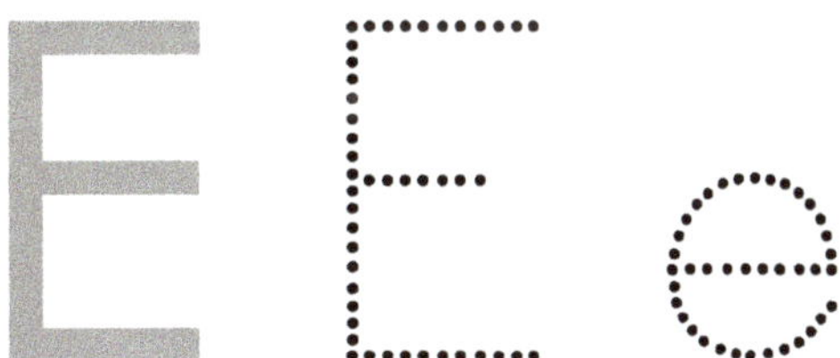

WOW! THIS IS A LOT OF FUN!

After they set up the tent and chairs, they
built a *Fire* to roast some marshmallows.

Wow! This is a lot of *Fun*.

The words *Fire* and *Fun* start with the letter

DO YOU LIKE HOT DOGS AND HAMBURGERS?

And they also cooked…hotdogs, hamburgers, and popped popcorn on the fire. They were very Grateful for everything and had a Great time.

"Do you like hotdogs and hamburgers?" asks Daniel the Dragon.

The words *Grateful* and *Great* start with the letter

All of a sudden, it started to
rain…so they hurried inside the
tent. They grabbed what they
could with their *Hands*.

"*Hurry!*" Daniel said.

The words *Hurry* and *Hands*
start with the letter

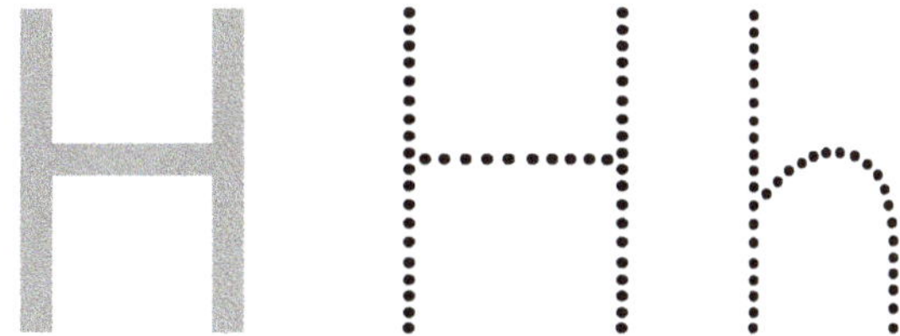

OH NO, THE LOGS ARE WET!
I'M A DRAGON, AND DRAGONS CAN BREATHE FIRE FROM THEIR MOUTH.
IDEA.
THANK YOU DANIEL.
YEAH!
HORRAY!

The next day, when they all got up, it was cold and wet, so Daniel had an idea. "I'm a dragon, and dragons can breathe fire from their mouths."

The whole family was clapping. Daniel saved the day.

HI NEVAEH!
HI NOAH!
HI

In Daniel's next adventure you will
be introduced to the new additions
to the Anderson Family, as they
decided to adopt a boy and a girl.

BYE FOR NOW

FOLLOW DANIEL'S NEXT ADVENTURES WITH HIS FAMILY, THE ANDERSONS, AS WE TRAVEL THE COUNTRY.
WE WILL CONTINUE TO LEARN THE LETTERS OF THE ALPHABET AND THEN HIS NEXT ADVENTURES AS DANIEL GETS ANOTHER IDEA "TO TRAVEL THE WORLD AND LEARN THE REST OF THE ALPHABET."
ALSO, YOU WILL BE ABLE TO LEARN INTERESTING FACTS ABOUT EACH AREA CALLED "DANIEL'S FUN FACTS" IN THE FOLLOWING TWO BOOKS. THIS WILL BE EDUCATIONAL AND INSPIRING TO THE CHILREN YOU READ IT TO.

Keep following the adventures of Daniel
the Dragon as we learn the alphabet
as he travels around the country.

Daniel says, "See you next time.
As we continue, can you think of
words that start with the letter I?"

About the Author

Randy Pagel has been drawing since he was about six years old. He was always interested in art at an early age. Randy started drawing comic pages at an early age and eventually started to paint in a variety of mediums including pencil, watercolor, ink, oil paints, and acrylic paints. Randy loves painting nature scenery and wildlife. It came very natural at a young age, and he had no previous schooling in this area.

Randy has taught art for a while mainly to friends and family, and he loves helping people learn. It is very rewarding. Randy is now in the process of having art shows to get his paintings exposed to the public.